THE WORLD'S CITIES

NEW YORK

CREDITS

Series Editor: Nicolas Wright
Series Designer: Kris Flynn
Picture Researcher: Kathy Brandt

Text by Chris Maynard and Gail Rebuck

Commissioned Photographs by
Peter Semler

Published by Chartwell Books Inc., A
Division of Book Sales Inc., 110 Enterprise
Avenue, Secaucus, New Jersey 07094

Produced by Theorem Publishing Limited,
71/73 Great Portland Street, London W1N 5DH
for Marshall Cavendish Books Limited

Printed in Great Britain

First printing 1978

ISBN 0 89009 160 9

THE WORLD'S CITIES

NEW YORK

CHARTWELL
BOOKS INC.

CONTENTS

Introduction to New York

Cities can be difficult places to come to grips with. Some require painstaking research and are best sampled in small doses; others seem to invite a more leisurely exploration. But not New York. Here is a city that requires no preliminary politeness, no careful reconnoitering before plunging in.

For visitors lucky enough to arrive by sea, like countless immigrants before them, the way to New York takes them directly past the 300 foot-high Statue of Liberty. The monument dominates the searoads and lets foreign travellers know that not only have they reached the New World, but that they have also arrived at a place where seemingly everything is done on a grand scale. A quick glance across the harbour is proof enough. The view ahead is of a sheer wall of concrete and glass—the towering skyscrapers of Lower Manhattan.

But the plunging canyons that intersect the buildings and lead the eye to the streets below are the key to another New York. The teeming streets tell a different story; the story of a city so diverse that it almost defies description. New York is the home of every kind of group, every kind of individual and manages to cater for every kind of taste.

Although the city is a conglomeration of five boroughs; the Bronx, Brooklyn, Queens, Staten Island and Manhattan, it is usually only the latter that people have in mind when they think of New York. In a very real way, Manhattan is indeed the heart and soul of the city. Here, like nowhere else, one is plunged into the excitement and exhilarating energy for which the city is renowned.

Manhattan is as easy to navigate as a sheet of graph paper. The majority of the city streets are laid out in a simple grid, each square of which is called a block, in which there are but two kinds of thoroughfares; streets (which run east to west) and avenues (which run north to south). The dividing line of east from west is Fifth Avenue which runs from Washington Square in Greenwich Village all the way to Harlem in the north. As a rough rule of thumb, north-south distances can be calculated by the fact there are 20 blocks to the mile.

Now for the exceptions: Broadway, which follows the path of an old Indian track and runs the entire length of Manhattan, meanders diagonally across the island from the southeast to the northwest. In the area south of 14th Street, New York's history triumphs over the logic of the grid system and the streets here become the jumble that most visitors from Europe used to the confusion of their own cities, will find familiar.

New York probably has a greater number of distinct neighbourhoods than any other city in the world. Not only can they be classified into categories such as working class, middle class and rich, or financial, shopping and entertainments, but also according to the dozens of different nationalities that live in the city. In Manhattan, the standard way to recognize that you have crossed from one ethnic neighbourhood into another is by the menus of restaurants. Nor are these the sort of menus you encounter in the rest of the United States, where a hamburger isn't fit to serve unless smothered in adjectives, and even the plainest slab of starch is qualified by at least a paragraph of ecstatic praise. New York menus are the genuine article, right down to the uncompromising spelling of unpronounceable ethnic dishes.

This book with its fascinating collection of hitherto largely unpublished photographs will show just what it is that makes New York America's most effervescent city and gives the place its world-wide reputation.

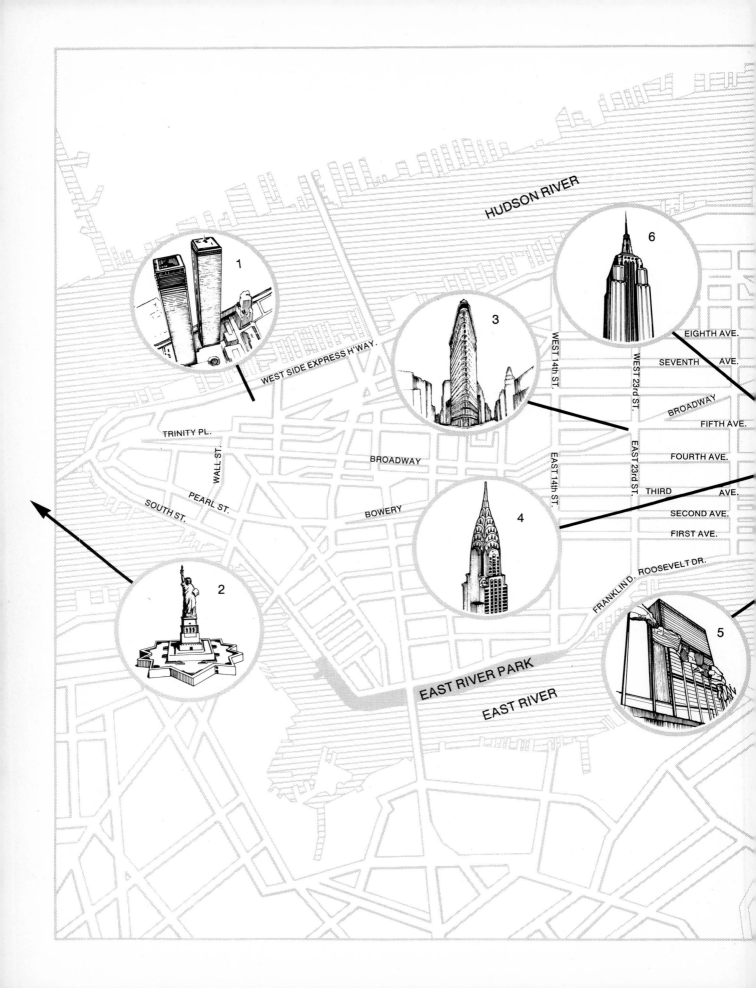

HUDSON RIVER

1

WEST SIDE EXPRESS H'WAY.

3

6

EIGHTH AVE.

SEVENTH   AVE.

WEST 14th ST.

WEST 23rd ST.

BROADWAY

FIFTH AVE.

TRINITY PL.

BROADWAY

FOURTH AVE.

WALL ST.

EAST 23rd ST.

PEARL ST.

BOWERY

4

EAST 14th ST.

THIRD   AVE.

SOUTH ST.

SECOND AVE.

FIRST AVE.

2

FRANKLIN D. ROOSEVELT DR.

5

EAST RIVER PARK

EAST RIVER

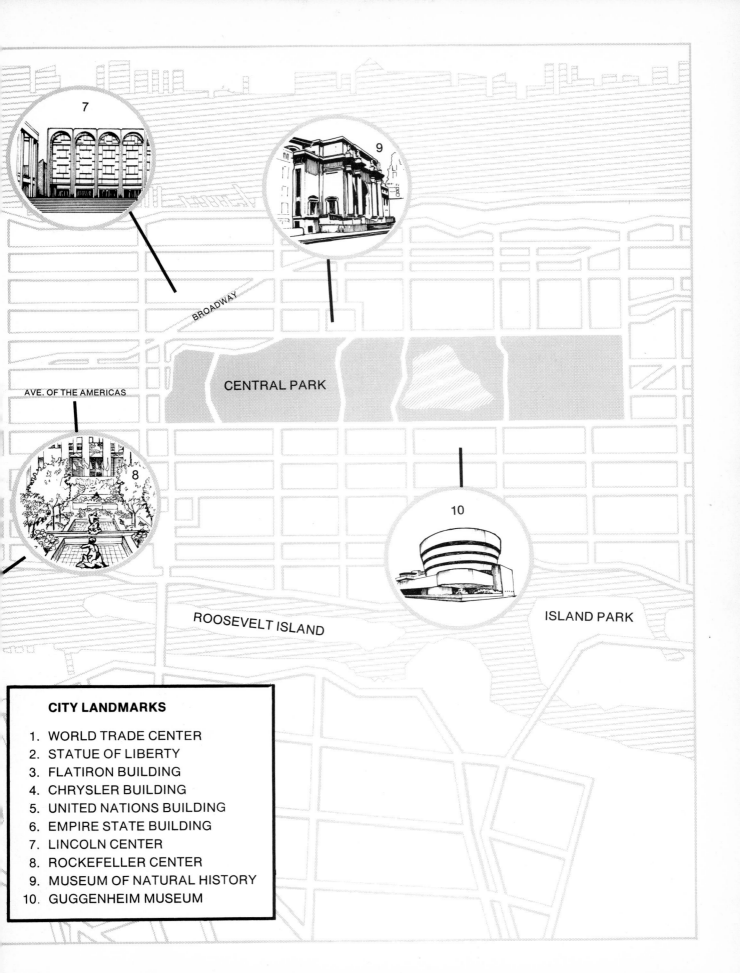

BROADWAY

AVE. OF THE AMERICAS

CENTRAL PARK

ROOSEVELT ISLAND

ISLAND PARK

CITY LANDMARKS

1. WORLD TRADE CENTER
2. STATUE OF LIBERTY
3. FLATIRON BUILDING
4. CHRYSLER BUILDING
5. UNITED NATIONS BUILDING
6. EMPIRE STATE BUILDING
7. LINCOLN CENTER
8. ROCKEFELLER CENTER
9. MUSEUM OF NATURAL HISTORY
10. GUGGENHEIM MUSEUM

New York Past and Present

New York's history is very recent. The only great tradition is construction. Yet very little of the city's beginnings have been physically preserved for the place is continuously rebuilding itself. As the natives are fond of saying, 'New York would be a great place to live if they ever finished building it'.

New York owes its existence to the sea. It possesses the finest deepwater harbour on the east coast of America and has long been the principal port of the United States for both trade and immigration.

Though Italian and Portuguese explorers were already nosing around New York harbour as early as the 16th century, it was the Dutch who founded the first colony here. In 1629, they established a small settlement at the southernmost tip of Manhattan, on a plot of land they purchased from the Algonquin Indians for a mere 60 guilders (about 24 dollars).

From the outset, New Amsterdam, as the settlement was christened, was run as a commercial enterprise. Administered for the Dutch West India Company by a succession of governors, its chief reason for existence was profit through trade – a business maxim New Yorkers have faithfully clung to ever since.

The venture was a success and the steady flow of beaver and otter skins attracted an equally steady flow of new settlers. By 1660, some 300 houses had already been built and land speculation, still a contemporary practice, was rife.

From the start, the settlement attracted an unruly populace. Even the famous tyrannical governor, Peter Stuyvesant, was reduced to issuing futile directives decrying the excessive drinking and general low-life of his citizens. However, his task was abruptly terminated in 1664 when two warships under the command of the Duke of York, brother of King Charles II of England, sailed into the harbour. The resistance put up by the 10,000 colonists was anything but fierce and the English captured the city without firing a shot.

The colony was renamed New York in honour of James, the Duke of York, and the inhabitants settled down to being loyal British subjects: a fickle loyalty as events a century later were to prove.

Almost nothing survives to mark the original 17th-century Dutch colony save the cramped layout of the streets of Lower Manhattan and a few place names such as Brooklyn (coming from Breukelen or marshland), Harlem, Stuyvesant Street and the Bowery. This last name derives from the small Dutch farms called *bouweries* that once dotted the countryside to the north of Wall Street.

Wall Street itself marks the path of the wooden wall that ran from the East River to the Hudson and defended New Amsterdam from northern attack. However, it was never much of a deterrent to the Indians who preferred canoeing on the river to tramping overland. Anyway, the European settlers made a habit of ripping out sections for firewood! The wall was pulled down by the English in 1699 and

The pulse of New York is the thunder of its traffic. The restless energy reaches a fevered crescendo at major junctions, such as here at Times Square.

became a street. Nearly a century later, in 1792, a group of traders met here at the Tontine coffee house, establishing a regular market to facilitate the buying and selling of government securities. Like most historic sites, this first home of the New York Stock Exchange was pulled down long ago. Today it is commemorated by a wall plaque.

Perhaps the only real vestige of the Dutch presence in New York is the Bowling Green Park, a tiny plot of land at the foot of lower Broadway. The Dutch colonists paid a nominal rent of one peppercorn a year to graze their cattle here. Later, the site was turned into the city's first public park. A statue of George III stood here until the War of Independence when it was melted down into musket balls and aimed at his troops.

This was the third and last time that New York changed masters. Though British troops managed to occupy the city and drive out Washington and his army, mysterious fires during the time of their occupation razed at least a third of the city to the ground. When the British withdrew in 1783, they left a much ruined New York behind. It was rebuilt virtually overnight and for one brief year in 1785, even acted as the first capital of the United States.

There are still one or two relics of the revolutionary era of New York's history that remain intact. One, Dyckman House (Broadway & West 204th St), is the only surviving farmhouse on the whole of Manhattan. Although it was built in the 1780s it mirrors the style used by wealthy farmers of the century before, being a broad solid-looking structure of stone and wood with a peculiarly long, sloped roof.

During the years of the British presence in New York, most buildings were faithful copies of English Georgian styles. Almost all are long gone, victims of the city's notorious nonstop efforts to destroy its past, save for St Paul's Chapel, a very English-looking church built in 1766 at the corner of Broadway and Fulton.

At the time of the War of Independence, the population of New York was approximately 20,000 people. By 1800 it had risen to 60,000 and 20 years later, it reached 120,000 making it the biggest city in the United States. Sixty years after that it had multiplied another ten times. However, the greatest years of expansion did not even begin until the mid-19th century.

The city grew at an incredible pace, overflowing the crowded area of Lower Manhattan, spilling northward along the island. Today, as a general rule, older buildings are concentrated at the southern end of the city while the newer ones occupy the area above 14th Street, the geographical dividing line between Lower and Midtown Manhattan.

Left: Gracie Mansion, the official residence of New York's mayor, is set in the pleasant greenery of Carl Shurz Park. The mansion's 18th century elegance offers a marked contrast to the city jungle its occupants are elected to manage.
Below: This quaint wooden building at the tip of Battery Park is the landing stage of the Staten Island Ferry.

But like any rule, this one has exceptions. In the late 18th century, wealthy New Yorkers who sought to escape from the bustle of the city in the surrounding countryside, built themselves mansions further north on the island. At the far end of what today is East 88th Street stands Gracie Mansion. This large, white-frame building was built in 1799 and is the traditional home of New York's mayors. At the very northern tip of Manhattan, at 161st Street, stands the Morris-Jumel Mansion. Originally erected in 1765 and extensively restored around 1810, this house was once located deep in the country. Today, the two buildings are the sole remains of the great 18th-century country homes that were once scattered around Manhattan.

A rare sight in New York is a building with a history. This clapboard church is a reminder of the days when wood, not steel and glass, was the city's main building material.

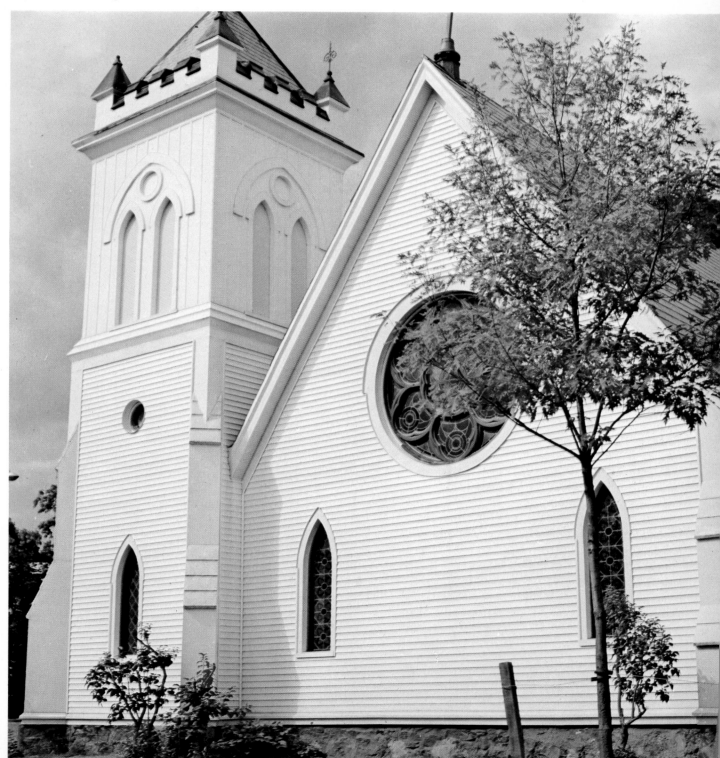

Left: The looming pile of St Patrick's Cathedral, a design inspired by Cologne Cathedral, on Fifth Avenue was built between 1858 and 1879 to serve New York's growing Roman Catholic population.

The Fraunces Tavern at the corner of Pearl and Broad streets is one of the oldest buildings in the city with a non-religious history: it still serves food and drink today. The Tavern's original claim to fame was that George Washington wished his troops farewell from here after the War of Independence. They were deceived, for he returned a few years later to be the country's first president – and its new Commander-in-Chief.

Not far away is Trinity Church, a fully-fledged gothic cathedral erected in 1846 on the site of a church of the same name, which was cleared away to make room for the newer building. Today it is surrounded by a lush green churchyard occupying the block between Broadway and Trinity Place. The site is over-shadowed by the nearby skyscrapers of the World Trade Center and the Chase Manhattan Plaza. South of Trinity Church on Beaver Street is the city's oldest, and still one of its finest restaurants, Delmonico's. Its contribution to the stability of the Stock Exchange is as considerable as any financial institution in the neighbourhood.

As one moves uptown, the financial district gradually merges with the political administration of New York; not by any means an incompatible arrangement. Here, south of Foley Square, are City Hall, the Municipal Building (the office of the city's administration), and the main courthouses. The present City Hall (it is the third) between Broadway and Park Row dates from 1811. It was built in the classical European tradition, but later modified to suit simpler, more democratic New World tastes. This style has since become known as 'American Federal'. The nearby City Hall Park is an expanse of green with a very chequered history, having at various times been the scene of riots, a public execution site, a madhouse and a graveyard.

The City Hall dates from the start of a boom period in New York's history when ideas and styles of building were imported from Europe in a wholesale way. The steady stream of immigrants brought with them the traditions and styles they had known at home. While they, for the most part, were too poor to build for themselves, they provided a pool of skilled talent that could realize the extravagant dreams of the rich who during the early decades of the 19th century, were beginning to discover Europe and acquire a greed for all its cultural trappings.

Right: This view of Trinity Church has hardly changed in 80 years. It was nearly as closely framed by the canyon-like gorge that is Wall Street in the 1890s (*below*) as it is today (*above*).

New Yorkers returned home fired with the thought of building their own Italian palaces, French chateaux, neo-gothic follies and every conceivable variation of classical Greek, Roman (even Egyptian) masterpieces. Houses and public buildings of any and every style were erected; Roman next to Victorian, both facing something Venetian. Often all three were combined in the same building. With complete disregard for the centuries of history and the diverse cultures that were being sandwiched in this way, the rich of Manhattan set about building.

For reasons of their own, the rest of the city's population were not slow to join the rich in their never-ending task of transforming Manhattan. Repeated outbreaks of fire and yellow fever in the narrow, overcrowded streets of the older parts of the city were a tremendous incentive for people to move uptown to newer and more fashionable neighbourhoods. Also, newly arrived immigrants tended to settle in the old, low-rent areas and drive out the earlier inhabitants who were appalled at the prospect of living next door to babbling foreigners.

Left: The rich of late 19th-century New York, and there were plenty of them, lived in ostentatious splendour in massive brownstone mansions along Fifth Avenue – then dubbed 'Millionaire's Row'.
Below: The narrow, neo-Georgian houses of Greenwich Village lend it the colourfully chaotic charm for which it is renowned.

This pattern of ever-shifting neighbourhoods has been characteristic throughout New York's history. It continues to this day.

Greenwich Village and the Bowery sprouted during the 1820s to house the expanding population from downtown. However, the utterly unplanned growth of New York that had so far been the rule was at last coming to an end. In 1807 the City Councillors appointed a group of commissioners to tackle the problem of the city's growth. They eventually devized a geometrically planned grid system of avenues (running north to south) and streets (running east to west) on the basis of which the rest of the island was to be surveyed and laid out.

One not unconsidered result of the new grid system was an explosive real estate boom. In the ensuing speculation, numerous New Yorkers pocketed small fortunes, among them Jacob Astor, the millionaire, who is reputed to have claimed on his deathbed that, had he been able to relive his life, he would snap up every available inch of land in Manhattan.

The opening of New York's first railway, the Harlem Railroad, in 1831, contributed to the city's rapid expansion by linking such small outlying villages as Bloomingdale, Yorkville and Harlem with the lower portion of Manhattan and adding them to the list of potential development sites. By now, great sections of the island were being measured out in block lots that were being built on as quickly as men and material could be brought to the site.

The feverish activity was fuelled by an astonishing population growth that in the 30 years prior to 1850 saw the city more than quadruple in size. Every ship that arrived in the harbour seemed to disgorge a stream of immigrants. In one year in the mid-1820s, some 22,000 Irish alone disembarked.

The majority of the newly arrived were next to penniless. They settled either in the crowded and squalid slums of the old downtown areas or else squatted in marshy, mosquito-ridden land in shanty towns that stretched toward the area later to become Central Park. The contrast between their misery and the elegant town houses going up around Washington Square could not have been more extreme, yet it well reflects the air of confusion and social upheaval that marked New York's expansion.

Throughout the first half of the 19th century, the major buildings erected in New York were all copied from one kind of European design or another and were usually executed in marble or the much-loved brownstone. But by the 1850s, a new and more functional style of building began to appear. The real estate boom in the city created such perennial shortages and delays that speed was everything when putting up a building. If corners could be cut by building simply and keeping decorations down to a minimum, then they were sure to be taken. In any case, there seemed little reason why department stores, offices and warehouses had to be elaborately dressed!

Above: The heyday of Manhattan's docks is past. With the steady shift of port activity to New Jersey, great tracts of waterfront have been left to decay slowly. Where street traffic has been siphoned off by expressways, whole neighbourhoods have been isolated.
Left: The 'El', a steam train running on elevated tracks, was part of New York's first rapid transit system begun in the 1870s to ease downtown traffic congestion.
Right: In later years, the line was electrified.

Simultaneously, American love of gadgetry and labour-saving devices was being applied to building methods. In particular, prefabricated sections and cast-iron structural skeletons helped to make building techniques far more efficient. They also introduced a distinct native style of architecture, the cast-iron building. What perhaps most appealed to New Yorkers was that these buildings not only were easy to erect but could be just as easily dismantled and reassembled elsewhere.

Cast-iron construction caused a major revolution in architecture. It did away with the need for sturdy walls and massive supporting columns and allowed much wider and longer window spaces. One of the most famous of the new buildings was the Haughwout Building (1857) at Broadway and Broome Street. Supposedly the first-ever office building with elevators, it was a direct ancestor of New York's best-known invention – the skyscraper.

A reaction to Manhattan's pell-mell expansion set in during the years immediately prior to the Civil War. Led by the *Evening Post,* a growing section of the public began campaigning for a check to the mindless growth spawned by the grid layout of the city. Commercial building was felt to be devouring every last inch of the island without the slightest consideration for the people living there. The need for recreational amenities resulted in the establishment of a commission that included, among others, the writer Washington Irving and the newspaper editor and poet William Bryant.

The outcome of their work was the setting aside of some 840 acres of parkland right in the middle of Manhattan. Designed by Olmstead & Vaux, Central Park was begun in 1859 and finished 20 years later. It was laid out with painstaking attention to detail and when complete, included ponds, meadows, paths to ride and walk on and even a zoo.

Above: The advertisement that became a landmark; the inveterate chain-smoker of Times Square has been puffing away for years.
Right: In the building boom of the late 19th century, thousands of cheap apartment blocks were erected all over the city. To save money and space, iron fire escapes were slung over the front of the buildings.

18

Right: The Statue of Liberty, the symbol embodying the hopes and ideals of a young nation, stands facing out to sea in New York harbour.

Far right: The Staten Island Ferry, long famous as the cheapest ride in New York, offers a scenic cruise across the Upper Bay from the tip of Lower Manhattan, past the Statue of Liberty to the borough of Staten Island.

While the Civil War had a devastating impact on the south of the United States, for New York it was a time of unchecked growth. Property values doubled between 1861 and 1865, railroads and banks prospered and the Stock Exchange, ever a faithful barometer of the times, boomed. New buildings mushroomed and Fifth Avenue became transformed into a two-mile boulevard of mansions known locally as 'Millionaire's Row'.

By now, the crowding in Manhattan had generated enough pressure for the population to start spilling across the river to Brooklyn and Queens, areas which were fast losing their country status and becoming sprawling dormitory suburbs, although it was not until 1898 that Manhattan and the outlying boroughs of the Bronx, Staten Island, Queens and Brooklyn were joined to form Greater New York, now the largest city in the world. The need to link them with Manhattan was acute and a series of bridges across the East River was begun; the most famous of them all was the Brooklyn Bridge. Begun in 1867, it took 16 years to build. People at the time marvelled at its twin gothic towers of masonry and its single, cable-hung central span arching gracefully across the river; they recognized it with pride as being a symbol of America's enormous energy and enterprise.

As a centennial birthday gift from France to the United States, and a token of the longstanding friendship between the two nations, the idea of a gigantic Statue of Liberty, embodying the American ideals of democracy and freedom, was conceived. The French sculptor, F. A. Bartholdi, was sent to New York. One glance at the city's harbour decided his site. The statue was to be placed on a little island off Lower Manhattan but looking out towards the mouth of the harbour – a perpetual welcome to all who arrived by sea.

Bartholdi returned to France and cast the outer skin of the statue in copper sheeting; it was supported by an inner skeleton of steel designed by Gustave Eiffel (famous for the tower in Paris). In 1885 the statue was shipped to America and, in October of that year, officially unveiled by President Cleveland. The statue depicts the Goddess of Liberty clothed in flowing robes. Held high in her right hand is a torch symbolizing liberty while the left hand holds the Declaration of Independence inscribed on a tablet. At her feet lie broken shackles, symbols of defeated tyranny. The statue and its base stand more than 300 feet high and together weigh some 225 tons. Inside is an elevator and a set of stairs allowing access to the viewing platform in her crown. As an idea of the scale of the Statue, the length of the right arm alone is 42 feet.

Despite this grand statement, New York was still suffering from real and urgent problems. If the spread to the suburbs represented one solution to overcrowding, equally inventive alternatives were being found within the constricted area of Manhattan itself. The most significant innovation to deal with the city's housing shortage was the apartment block. First introduced in 1869 by Richard Hunt, the idea was an immediate triumph. One of the earliest and most successful apartment buildings was The Dakota, a sprawling luxury block with a deliberate Renaissance chateau-look, overlooking Central Park at 72nd Street and built in 1884. It has always been one of the most fashionable addresses in the city, particularly among noted people in the arts.

Apartments were a housing solution for the rich and middle classes; but for the poor a different sort of building was devised – the tenement. The first were erected as early as 1835. As Louis Mumford writes in his book *Sticks and Stones*, they were a means of 'producing congestion, raising ground-rents, and satisfying in the worst possible way the need of the new immigrants for housing'. By the late 1870s, a standardized tenement design, known as the dumb-bell, had emerged; shaped like a dumb-bell, the interiors were so narrow that the flow of fresh air was virtually impossible. Some survive to this day in the crumbling districts of the lower East Side and in the Bronx.

Left: Behind the glittering facade, acute social problems beset the city of New York. The extremes of wealth and poverty are never more than a few blocks apart.
Right: The scale of the past and of the present; scarcely a century ago St Patrick's Cathedral overshadowed mid-town Manhattan. Today, skyscrapers dwarf its ornate splendour.

By now, the transformation of the New York skyline was gathering momentum. The technique of erecting steel-framed buildings, combined with elevators and improved heating and ventilation systems, heralded a radically new concept in architecture. It provided the ideal solution to New York's chronic shortage of land, finding room in the sky where none existed on the ground. Although the idea of building tall was not new (complaints about the canyon-like streets of Lower Manhattan had been heard since the 1850s) technological limitations had previously restricted buildings to approximately five storeys. Now, with the advent of steel-frame buildings, the sky was quite literally the limit.

One of the first buildings to possess the characteristic slimness and soaring elegance of a skyscraper was the Flatiron Building, erected in

1902 on 23rd Street at the corner of Broadway and Fifth Avenue. Others soon followed turning the city into the forest of steel and concrete for which it is world famous.

Early skyscrapers, such as the Chrysler, Daily News and Woolworth Buildings, still kept a certain amount of decoration on their façades but since then, simpler and more stripped-down designs have become the rule. Today, the 'International Style' predominates. Its characteristic features are great unadorned rectangular slabs of glass and aluminium or steel.

Since World War II, New York's population has reached a plateau and now hovers fairly steadily around the figure of eight million. But this overall stability hides a tremendous shift in the make-up of the population. Throughout the 1950s and 1960s, a mass exodus from the inner city to the suburbs took place. Predominantly middle class and white familites moved away and their place was largely taken by a massive influx of poor southern blacks and Puerto Ricans. The results of this shift are very marked indeed, for the 1,700,000 population of Manhattan is now more than ever divided between the very rich and the very poor, each in their own ghettos.

The most visible signs of this imbalance are the grim decaying slum areas of Harlem, the south Bronx and parts of Brooklyn. Though unlikely to be visited by the average tourist, they serve as a stark reminder that New York is not all flashiness and glamour.

However, the problems that haunt New York are shared in some degree by many of the greatest metropolises. In New York they are significantly offset by the vibrantly cosmopolitan life the city attracts. Perhaps it is just a cruel paradox that a city with such seemingly insoluble social problems should also be one of the most alluring, vibrant and exciting places in the world.

Left: Nightfall, and the city becomes transformed into a world of glittering lights. The tempo of life picks up again after dusk and a new world of excitement beckons.
Below: A token will take you anywhere into the tiled underworld of New York's subway system; nowadays half-hidden beneath the fantastic hieroglyphics of spray-on graffiti.

Reaching for the Sky

At the turn of the 20th century the combination of a massive population explosion, rocketing real estate prices and revolutionary developments in the construction industry (not to mention big business's hunger for prestige) resulted in a breathtakingly simple solution to the overcrowding problems of Manhattan. Americans began building up higher and higher creating the world's most renowned skyline.

The history of the skyscraper is hard to disentangle. An acknowledged forerunner is the Haughwout Building (488 Broadway), a department store built from prefabricated cast iron sections, completed in 1857, and boasting the first fully operational 'elevator'. One of the earliest and most distinctive skyscrapers is the Flatiron Building (1902). Built to match exactly the tapering corner lot of Broadway and Fifth Avenue, the aptly named Flatiron rises 20 storeys. While the exterior has neo-rennaissance pretensions, the inner construction, a firm steel frame, strikes a new note. This building method set a new style to which there seemed to be no limits. Ten years later, New York saw the towering 60 storey Woolworth Building (233 Broadway) with its fancy neo-gothic style tiered crown, being completed.

But the real boom in skyscrapers came with the roaring 1920s. The stunning art deco style of the Chrysler Building (42nd St and Lexington Ave) completed in 1930 and reaching 1048 feet to the tip of its spire is proof enough. The steel used in its construction is said to be the hardest ever forged. The 102 storeys of the Empire State Building (350 Fifth Ave), completed in 1931 with its seven miles of lift shafts and floor space capable of housing 20,000 workers, remained unequalled for nearly half a century. The 86th floor observation deck still gives a memorable view of New York.

Skyscrapers were sprouting faster than anyone had imagined. No-one disputed the force, power and energy of the single unit, its pride and exalted attitude, but the maze of streets below was becoming a living nightmare. In 1940, 14 years of planning came to fruition in the Rockefeller Center (Midtown, between Fifth & Sixth Ave). Thirteen buildings were erected around a central plaza on a 17 acre site. The landscaped walkways and plazas set out to prove that the human element could still be combined with a high rise, high density commercial precinct.

But it was only after World War Two with the use of materials such as glass and aluminium that the skyscraper became the delicate long slim structure that we recognise today. No more mixing of outward styles, but simply an elegant building standing alone, a symbol of the efficient, no-trimmings modern world. The United Nations (First Ave between 42nd and 48th St) completed in 1953, and designed by an international group of architects, relies heavily on these principles. Also noteworthy are the Manufacturers Hanover Trust Bank (510 Fifth Ave), a steel structure completed in 1954, covered by a glass curtain wall, revealing the inner workings to all passers-by; the Seagram Building (375 Park Ave), a sheath of brown glass set back from the street; and the stunning Number '9' West 57th St—a mirrored column which begins with a curve from ground level.

There have been criticisms too—the Pan Am Building (200 Park Ave), a 60 storey high slab of concrete with a now unused heliport on its flat roof, is said to have added too much traffic to the Grand Central complex without introducing any compensating amenities.

But perhaps the ultimate building in New York is the modestly

The view from the street in downtown Manhattan is one of soaring perspectives that threaten to overwhelm with their gigantic scale.

Left: The Flatiron Building takes its name from its resemblance to this widely used household utensil. Since 1902, it has been one of the most unusual-looking buildings in the city.

Below: The terraced central plaza of the Rockefeller Center is transformed from a skating rink in winter to an outdoor café in the summer.

Right: The name Rockefeller has never been synonymous with understatement. The statue of Atlas, here framed by the International Building – one of the 13 skyscrapers in the Rockefeller Center – might well be a symbol of the family's all-embracing business activities.

named World Trade Center with some nine million square feet of office space devoted to—world trade. Its twin, 1302 feet towers dwarf even the Empire State and from the observation deck there is a splendid view of the city and a panorama that, on a clear day, extends some 50 miles into the distance.

The New York skyline is certainly not a testimony to human responsibility and planning, but the sight of so many towers jostling to be seen cannot fail to take your breath away.

Left: Since 1975, the World Trade Center has captured the prize of Tallest-Building-in-New York; and it goes without saying that that includes the rest of the world. Incredible as it may seem, a mountain-climbing enthusiast actually scaled the building in the summer of 1977 – and was arrested for trespassing!

Above: The sloping flanks of 'No. 9' West 57th Street make this stunning skyscraper one of the most beautiful in the city.

Right: Clearly visible in the burnished facade of one skyscraper is the reflection of its neighbour directly opposite.

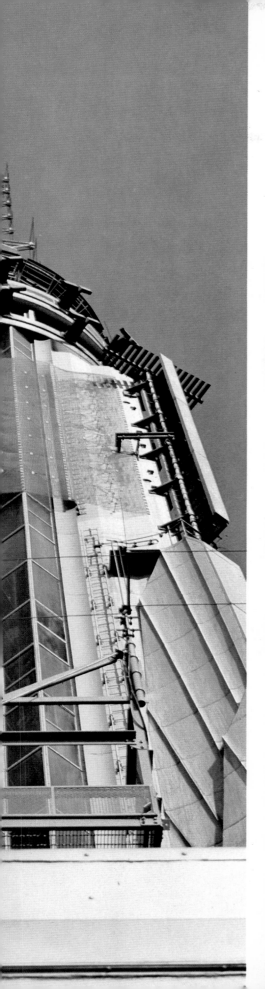

Far left: The Woolworth Building is one of the city's oldest skyscrapers.
Left: A view of the top of the Empire State Building, once the world's tallest skyscraper.
Below: The third highest skyscraper in New York is the Chrysler Building ornately Art Deco in design.

Serving to Please

No matter what you want to buy, no matter how obscure your tastes, you will be satisfied in New York. Although the city is tottering on the brink of bankruptcy, evidence of wealth and luxury abounds.

It might appear masochistic to have your competitors all around you, but New York shopkeepers seem to have a marked preference for this kind of set up. 'Diamond Row' (along 47th St) is the market for 80 per cent of the entire US trade; the shops are simply furnished though crammed with spectacular jewels. The Flower Market (along 28th St) houses more than 1,000 florists, while a third of all the clothes sold in the US are manufactured in the Garment District (a 30 block area between Fifth & Seventh Ave, 28th & 38th St). The traffic here is a nightmare of overloaded clothes rails whizzing past, driven by young apprentices. The Fur District handles 90 per cent of America's furs.

For books and handicrafts visit Greenwich Village – although the midtown bookstores of Brentanno's, Scribners and Doubleday should not be missed; small art galleries abound and crowd the ten block area of Madison Avenue around the Whitney Museum.

For curios and exotic spices visit Chinatown; for pastas, Little Italy on the East Side. New Yorkers have an obsession about food; the city is a gourmet's paradise of delicatessens – don't miss Zabars (Broadway & 80th St) for a cornucopia of cheeses and cold cuts.

But the wholesale districts and neighbourhood shops are only one side of the picture. In New York, everything is big, the variety is stunning, and ease of access is of the utmost importance. Hence the popularity of the department store, a style perfected in New York, gigantic complexes which offer a wealth of top quality goods.

Bloomingdales (Lexington Ave, 59th St) is famed for its superlative household department and food store. For women's clothes, visit Saks (Fifth Ave, 50th St) to find boutiques devoted to all the great names in design; for bargain hunters, try Alexanders (next door to Bloomingdales). Macy's (Broadway, 35th St) with its excellent toy department, is the biggest store of them all – and in New York being biggest is just as important as being best. FAO Schwarz (Fifth Ave, 58th St) carries nothing but toys; Abercrombie & Fitch (Madison Ave, 45th St) excels in sporting equipment; for men's clothes, visit the renowned Brooks Bros (Madison Ave, 44th St). But for gimmicks, extravagances, and outrageous gadgets (the world is surely a better place since the invention of the square egg maker!) drop into Hammacher Schlemmer (145 E 57th St).

From the great shops to the grand hotels, size and opulence still predominates. A private luxury bathroom, water or vibrating bed, colour TV, air conditoning and special iced water taps and bar are standard features in most top class hotels. The Plaza is perhaps the grandest in the city, run in the European tradition, where the staff remember the guest's name. Traditional sumptuous decor enjoyed by the élite who stay there also characterizes the St Regis Sheraton. The renowned Waldorf Astoria and elegant Regency Hotel with its Louis XIV style suites both rank among the greats. Newcomers, such as the New York Hilton, with its 2150 rooms built in an international luxury style, exist side by side with the famed Algonquin, steeped in the culture of the 'Round Table' dinners, where 'personalities' still enjoy cocktails in the pannelled lobby.

But just as vast department stores exist alongside the smaller shops, so the grand hotels vie with the smaller establishments. The Chelsea Hotel breathes an air of gentility from another age with its fancy wrought iron balconies and fading gothic style.

The greatest shopping street of them all, Fifth Avenue, is crowded with exclusive boutiques, expensive department stores, bookshops, jewellers and toyshops.

Food has the status of a minor religion in this city; and for many New Yorkers, paradise is the neighbourhood 'deli'. Wherever you go, there are people talking food, thinking food, selling food and, above all, eating it. For many, the ultimate in *al fresco* dining is at a street corner vending cart.

Below: The jostling weekday crowds on Fifth Avenue make leisurely window shopping a nightmare. A quiet Sunday stroll is the only way to take in the sights at a relaxed pace.

Left: The Waldorf-Astoria on Park Avenue, with a guest list straight out of *Who's Who,* is the ultimate in the grand hotel tradition.
Below: The Lexington, with more than 800 rooms, epitomizes a modern, unpretentious style of hotel.
Right: The magnificent Plaza Hotel, overlooking the southern end of Central Park, recreates a grand European tradition with its imposing, chateau-style atmosphere.

Left: Neighbourhood restaurants may be as simple as this diner; but the tradition of fast food, served in huge portions, survives even here. *Below* and *right:* Shopping in New York ranges from the grand – Tiffany's is one of the most fashionable jewellers in the city – to the cheerful stalls of a street market. Orchard Street on the Lower East Side is a mecca for Sunday bargain hunters.

The Almighty Dollar

If there is any truth in the saying 'money makes the world go round', then New York wins an uncontested prize for the rate of its spin.

Although the city itself is in dire financial straits, nobody finds it strange that one of the greatest concentrations of wealth in the world should also be found here. Roughly one fifth of the 500 biggest businesses in America have their headquarters in New York. The financial district around Wall Street is a hive of banks, trust companies, insurance corporations, public utilities, railway and shipping concerns, stock brokers and exchanges. So great is the prestige of a Wall Street address that companies are willing to endure crippling rents of up to 600 dollars a square foot; the highest in the world as any superlative-loving New Yorker will hurry to let you know.

Here, in Lower Manhattan, the financial district faithfully preserves the original dimensions of New York. The narrow and hopelessly chaotic maze of streets traces out what were once 18th-century lanes and paths. During the day, the pavements are crammed with a solid phalanx of office workers who vanish uptown and to the suburbs at night, leaving the area eerily deserted.

Unlike the shopping and cultural heart of the city, which has moved north over the years to the midtown area between 14th Street and Central Park, the financial district still retains its links with the port—New York's traditional reason for existence. Though Manhattan is faced with vigorous competition from New Jersey, the port is still going strong and is easily the busiest in the country. Every year some 20 million tons of cargo pass through its 23 miles of harbour installations.

Yet for the distilleries, oil corporations, car manufacturers, airlines, publishing and broadcasting giants with no historical links with the port, midtown Manhattan acts as another centre of gravity. The broad boulevard of Park Avenue—divided by a neat centre lane of greenery—and the Avenue of the Americas (still called Sixth Avenue by the locals) are lined with the opulent steel and glass monuments that some of the most powerful and influential companies in the nation have built as their headquarters.

Here too is Madison Avenue, the street made famous by the advertizing trade; although few companies now have their addresses here. American advertizing developed the art of selling as big business in its own right; perhaps there is no better measure of its success than the raw figures of what is bought and sold annually in New York—an estimated 100 billion dollars worth of trade. Buying and selling, that is the preoccupying activity of most New Yorkers. Relatively few work in

The claim that 'what is good for business is good for America' is rarely as aptly expressed as in the smoked glass windows of this sleek limousine in the heart of the financial district.

manufacturing. The largest such industry, the garment business, employs about a quarter of a million people. It is easily overshadowed by the four million office workers who staff the financial, trade and service industries.

Yet the true nature of commercial New York is not to be found in the gleaming office blocks of the midtown giants. Tucked away inconspicuously throughout the city are tens of thousands of small, struggling entrepreneurs. The average size of a New York business is 15 people. Small may not be beautiful when compared to the plush elegance of the big and wealthy, but it is still very much the name of the commercial game.

Above: The littered floor of the New York Stock Exchange proclaims it the world's busiest. As many as 35 million shares a day have been traded here.

Left: If nothing else, the classical columns of the New York Exchange are a reminder that, in the 20th century, it too is very much a temple.

Right: Yet another of the great public monuments of the 19th century is the US Treasury Building, again reflecting New York's preference for dressing up financial institutions as classical Greek temples.

Above left: Typical of the Seventh
Avenue Garment District are the
delivery men who shuttle around the
neighbourhood towing trolleys
loaded with cloth and finished
clothes. On the empty return
journey, they push-ride the trolleys
with a reckless skill that has earned
them the name 'Seventh Avenue
aviators'.

Left: What the Garment District
handles today, America wears
tomorrow. Nearly a third of all the
clothes bought in the United States
originate here.

Right: The only subject that rivals
New Yorkers' preoccupation with
getting rich is the problem of staying
that way. The protection business is
a major industry here. In a city with
almost a quarter of a million reported
robberies a year (barely the tip of the
iceberg), people are obsessed with
alarms, locks, safes and burglar
defences of every kind.

Above: Kennedy International Airport is America's third largest port, land or sea, in the value of the goods that it handles. Millions of dollars of small costly items such as bullion shipments, diamonds and works of art pass through here daily.
Right: Where else but in the city which claims to be the world's richest would the biggest bank vault be found? The vaults beneath the Chase Manhattan Building are almost the size of a small football pitch and are protected by doors weighing some 40 tons.

Side by Side

Manhattan is a melting pot of nationalities. As early as the 17th century, more than a dozen different languages were spoken on the island. Undaunted by the arduous sea journey, the appalling food, brackish water, filth and frequent deaths, settlers from all over the world continued to flood into New York in search of a new beginning.

As late as a century ago, more than half the inhabitants of Manhattan had been born outside the USA. Each shipload fed a small community which jealously protected its traditions. These traditions blended together to form the New Yorker we know today, though the original communities still survive in tight groups all over the island.

Emigration to New York first acquired tidal proportions in the 19th century with the large influx of Irish fleeing political unrest and famine at home. By 1870, one fifth of the population of Manhattan was Irish. A little later, waves of Italian peasants arrived from Naples and Sicily, while Jews escaping from persecution in Eastern Europe also helped to swell the throng.

Needless to say feuds soon sprang up between the newcomers and the more established. Most noteworthy were the battles between the Irish, German and black communities. The Italians, on the other hand, tended to stick together; their close family ties engendering the notorious Mafia network. The Jewish community was perhaps the most ostracized, having to suffer both Catholic and Protestant dislike. Today, New York hosts nearly half a million Italians, some 200,000 Irish, 300,000 Germans and Austrians, and a Jewish population of more than two million.

At the turn of the century, the first blacks began to settle in Harlem, so named by Peter Stuyvesant after a town in the Netherlands. Previously a fine residential area, Harlem began to decline with the influx of immigrants from the south who arrived with little money and poor chances of finding decent jobs. The area decayed as unscrupulous landlords allowed apartments to become delapidated tenements in which high rents led to even further overcrowding. Today, violence and discontent is a daily feature in Harlem, and whites are definitely not welcome there. During the 1950s, Puerto Ricans began to settle in East Harlem, a colourful though again poor and badly decaying area of the city known more recently as Spanish Harlem. The combined population of blacks and Puerto Ricans in New York today numbers nearly three million.

Considerable evidence of different cultures can also be seen in downtown Manhattan. Moving north from the financial district, you soon reach Chinatown, crammed with authentic restaurants, tea houses and of course laundrys. Here, even the telephone boxes have pagoda roofs and are adorned with Chinese characters. Though at one time racked by virulent Tong feuds, the community of around 20,000 Chinese today lives in relative peace. The high spot of the year is the New Year celebration, a festival of dragons, lanterns and dancing.

A print of the scene that greeted new arrivals at Ellis Island recalls the hardships of their passage to a new life. At its peak, up to 8,000 immigrants a day, seven days a week, were cleared through the receiving station here.

Left: The look of the Old World transplanted to the new; here in Little Italy an old lady surveys the passing scene.
Below: Greenwich Village has traditionally been the focal point of America's bohemians.

Nearby in Little Italy, a similar national festival for San Gennaro, the patron saint of Naples, is held every year in September when a statue of the saint, covered in dollar bills, is paraded through the streets. In East Village, you will discover a real hodgepodge of races and creeds with Jewish delicatessens jostling with Greek markets and Italian pasta shops, interspersed with a variety of churches.

There is a small community of Hungarians between 70th and 78th Street along Second Avenue, and a Scandinavian conclave across the East River on Brooklyn Bay Ridge. The Irish are dispersed throughout the city although much in evidence on the green tinted occasion of St Patrick's Day in mid-March. The Greek Independence Day Parade takes place in April and the Puerto Ricans are out in force in June.

Other villages, not solely formed by ethnic groups, also exist in Manhattan. Greenwich Village and Chelsea are havens for artists and students complete with French style cafés and craft shops. The vast warehouses of the SoHo area (South of Houston St) make excellent studios for painters and aspiring film-makers and overspill into NoHo (it had to be North of Houston St!), an area more renowned for its art galleries and chic restaurants. On a more sombre note the Bowery, the 'skid-row' of Manhattan, is a miserable area of alcoholics, drop outs, doss houses and pawn shops.

Each community or village in New York is distinct. They are often closed to outsiders who can only peer at the cultural trappings. Perhaps the melting-pot image is the wrong one for New York. A fruit salad of peoples and cultures is more appropriate where the pieces, although mixed together, manage to stay very distinct.

Left: Chinatown flourishes in Lower Manhattan like some odd transplant from the Orient; but the pagoda phone box is a distinctly American touch.

Right: In recent years, the slums of Harlem have become the almost exclusive preserve of New York's black community.

Below: In the Lower East Side, European-style street markets, that once catered solely for the city's immigrant population, continue to flourish.

Below: The abandoning of the
Bowery for more fashionable areas
led this once bustling area to decline
and become the last refuge of the
city's all too numerous down-and-
outs.
Below right: The annual St Patrick's
Day Parade brings New Yorkers
claiming Irish descent out by the
thousands for a boisterous stroll
down Fifth Avenue.

Cultural New York

Culture can be measured in many different ways. Switch on a television set in New York and select a programme from one of 14 different stations or turn on the radio and flick through 40 broadcasts, including ten foreign language stations. Or else, walk along Broadway around Times Square through a district that contains more than 30 theatres; for museums and art galleries wander up Fifth Avenue or browse through some 40 odd small, private galleries and dealers along Madison Avenue between 74th and 84th streets and any number of others around the SoHo-Greenwich Village area.

Millions of dollars are made available to the arts every year in New York, most from private subscription. The city is by far the leading cultural centre in the United States. For music lovers, a visit to the famed Carnegie Hall (West 57th St & 7th Ave) is a must. The hall was built by Andrew Carnegie, the Scottish born steel millionnaire and is the former home of the New York Philharmonic. It is famous for its excellent acoustics. The present home of the Philharmonic is the giant arts complex known as the Lincoln Center. The six buildings that comprise it are visited by more than four million people people a year and house the New York State Theatre, the Opera House, the Vivian Beaumont Theatre, the Julliard School and a library and museum of the performing arts.

But New York does not only offer the fine arts. On a more popular level of culture there are also places such as Radio City Music Hall. Built as part of the Rockefeller Center in the 1930s, the main auditorium can seat up to 6200 people. Here, movies are shown along with a spectacular show that includes the Rockettes, a 36-strong precision-dancing chorus line, who to this day are Radio City's greatest attraction.

The New York Public Library on Fifth Avenue and 42nd Street houses more than seven and a half million volumes and has a priceless collection of rare manuscripts, while the Museum of the City of New York (Fifth Ave & 103rd St) traces the history of the city from its Dutch beginnings to the thriving metropolis it is today. A sample of the past can also be enjoyed at the Fraunces Tavern (Pearl St & Broad St) in Lower Manhattan. This tavern, now a restaurant, was first opened in 1762 and was witness to George Washington's farewell to his officers at the end of the War of Independence.

Museums abound in New York. The vast American Museum of Natural History, with more than 40 acres of floor space, is the biggest in the world. It contains an astounding collection of animal life and its exhibits portray each creature in its natural setting. A library, daily lectures and a splendid jewel collection—including the famous Star of India sapphire—are merely added attractions. The museum is a fascinating place showing everything from fossil skeletons to reconstructions of the South American rain forests.

The Metropolitan Museum of Modern Art (Fifth Ave & 84th St) which opened in 1880, is arguably the greatest museum in the country. It houses a collection of more than one million objects of art that span the entire 5000 years of civilized human culture. The Cloisters at Fort Tyron Park, is a branch of the Metropolitan that houses a splendid collection of medieval art.

The Frick Collection (East 70th St & Fifth Ave) is open to the public in Henry Frick's sprawling 19th-century mansion. It is a superlative collection of paintings, furniture and other furnishings. The Whitney Museum (Madison Ave & 75th St) covers the contemporary art scene from 1900 while the Museum of Modern Art (53rd and Fifth Ave) has a

The giant spiral seashell that is the Guggenheim Museum, houses a splendid permanent collection of over 4000 works of modern art.

collection of modern work in every medium from cinema to
photography and design. It is entirely financed by subscriptions and
public donations.

Occasionally, the buildings which house the art treasures are as
intriguing as the works themselves. One such place is the Guggenheim
Museum (Fifth Ave & 89th St) designed by the renowned architect
Frank Lloyd Wright. The museum is a strange looking cone of
concrete, rather similar to a spiral shell. Visitors walk through the
exhibit down a continuous ramp, starting at the roof and making their
way to ground level.

Below: The vast foyer of the World Trade Center is an ideal setting for art exhibitions.
Right: A view of the cylindrical interior of the Guggenheim reveals the spiralling ramp that winds from the top to the ground. Natural light floods down the central well from the glass-domed roof.
Below right: Outside the Chase Manhattan Plaza in the heart of the financial district stands the beautiful sculpture *Trees* by Debuffet. A Japanese water garden lies in the Plaza's sunken courtyard.

Left: Overlooking the central plaza and fountain of the Lincoln Center for the Performing Arts are the ten-storey arches of the Metropolitan Opera House. The Lincoln Center houses a philharmonic orchestra, a ballet company, two opera companies, a theatre, a music school and a magnificent library of the arts.
Below: The Gallery of Modern Art.

63

Left: The South Street Seaport Museum on the East River is one of the all too rare attempts to preserve something of New York's past. Here, a number of 19th-century sailing ships are moored.

Below: The vast brownstone front of the American Museum of Natural History, the largest of its kind in the world, overlooks west Central Park. Its exhibits range from natural history to outer space, diamonds, and ancient civilizations.

Right: The choice of cinema in New York is next to limitless. Here, in an advertisement for the updated version of King Kong, the great ape keeps abreast of changing times by unhesitatingly choosing the new World Trade Center, as opposed to the original film's Empire State Building.

A Sporting City

A Sunday stroll in Central Park will go a long way to dispelling the illusion that Americans are a nation of spectator sportsmen. The park roads, which are clogged with traffic during the week, are doubly choked with a swarm of determined joggers and cyclists; up to 50,000 cyclists alone come into the park on a busy weekend.

Physical fitness has, in recent years, become an intense national obsession and the weekend is peak time when the fitness cultists come out in full force. Nor do they go lacking for things to do since the list of sports facilities in Central Park verges on the encyclopaedic.

If jogging and cycling are not to your taste, you can choose boating, soccer, horseshoes, squash, baseball, football, field hockey, bird watching, model yachting, fishing, kite flying, lawn bowling, handball — the list goes on to include some 24 different sports and activities.

In winter, ponds are turned into outdoor skating rinks if the weather is cold enough and indoor rinks stand ready if it is not. Aside from the Central Park rinks, there is also an outdoor one in the Central Plaza of Rockefeller Center where piped music encourages the skaters.

Aside from the 800 acre expanse of Central Park, New York is not well supplied with places of greenery. True, there is the long tongue of Riverside Park running the length of the Upper West Side and Battery Park on the extreme southern end of the island, also the very beautiful Prospect Park in Brooklyn. But for the most part parks are afterthoughts to the city's main development. New York compensates to a degree with a number of so-called 'vest pocket parks'. Dotted around the city are odd little lots that have been set aside for people to sit and rest, and children to play. Here they are benches and potted shrubs; one park on 53rd Street even has an artificial waterfall.

The high temples of American sport are the big arenas such as Shea Stadium in Queens and Yankee Stadium in the Bronx where tens of thousands of fans regularly gather to watch football and baseball games. Of the two sports, perhaps baseball has the greater aura associated with it — although football pulls the bigger crowds. Yankee Stadium, for instance, even has a corner set aside for a monument to Babe Ruth, the homerun king of the 1920s. His record of 60 homeruns in a single season remained unbroken from 1927 to 1961.

Baseball is a relatively slow-moving game during which as much spectator energy goes into abusing the players and chatting with each other as into watching the game. The activity in the stands is nonstop with the fans acting as human chains to pass hotdogs and drinks along the bleacher rows. Halfway through the game an odd ritual occurs known as the seventh inning stretch. As one, the fans rise and begin yawning and stretching in the effort to recirculate the pooled blood on which they were sitting, back to the rest of their body.

Aside from the vast ball parks, there is also the famous Tennis Stadium at Forest Hills where professional and international tournaments are played. The highpoint of the tennis season comes in early September when the US Open Championships are held here. In the middle of Manhattan, at 33rd Street and Eighth Avenue, is the venerable Madison Square Gardens, an arena where every sport from track and field events to indoor bicycling, boxing, wrestling and even

Baseball, described by one English visitor as 'frantic cricket', is arguably one of America's greatest inventions. Here, caught in the act, a swinging batter strikes out.

The vast bowls of Shea Stadium *above*, and Yankee Stadium *below*, can each hold the population of a small city. They are the home grounds of New York's professional baseball and football teams.
Right: As if the term 'rat race' were not literal enough, New Yorkers by the thousands have donned sweat suits and taken to jogging around Central Park.

circuses are held. New York's professional basketball team, the Knickerbockers, play all their home games here as do the New York Rangers hockey team. Soccer, known throughout the rest of the world as football, has only recently become a popular sport in America. The city's professionals, the Cosmos, play at Downing Stadium on Randalls Island.

New York is also a thriving centre for horse racing. Thoroughbred events are held at the Belmont and Aqueduct tracks in Queens. The most important race of the year is the Belmont Stakes for three-year-olds, held every year in mid-June.

What could be more logical in a city as richly endowed with museums as New York than a museum to sport. Just such a place exists, the Boxing Hall of Fame at 120 West 31st Street. Here are photographs, fightbills and countless mementos of all the great boxers.

Three great American sports;
baseball, football and lifting hotdogs
to the mouth.

MADISON SQUARE GARDEN CENTER

Left and below: Madison Square Gardens from outside and within. In this great indoor stadium, professional boxing, hockey and basketball tournaments are regularly staged.
Below left: The sunken central plaza of Rockefeller Center is converted into an ice-skating rink in winter.

New York Off-Duty

Like everything else in New York, the pleasures that can be sampled here are not so much unrestricted as limitless in their range. The answer as to what New Yorkers do when they are not at work is, like the classic Yiddish joke, simply another question; namely, what do they not do?

Everybody loves a parade and few cities enjoy so many as New York. The tickertape procession through the narrow streets of Lower Manhattan is a long-established tradition and a standard welcome accorded to astronauts, sportsmen, popular politicians and returning heroes of every description. As the parade goes by, the windows of every stock-dealing institution in the district are opened to shower down long ribbons of tickertape and general office confetti by the ton.

Aside from these one-off occasions, there are a good dozen major parades that are annual events. The Polish community of the city takes to the streets every year at the beginning of October to proclaim its ethnic virility. The Irish take advantage of St Patrick's Day on 17 March to stage a similar display. However, the Irish presence in New York has acquired a certain legendary status of its own which results in the parade taking aboard a remakable quota of Jewish, Chinese, Puerto Rican, Italian and even English Irishmen, all happily proclaiming their suddenly remembered heritage with emerald green ties, hats and umbrellas. Even the white line down the centre of Fifth Avenue gets painted green for the day. To paraphrase a famous commercial, you don't have to be a New Yorker to be Irish – but it helps.

Hundreds of thousands of people turn out to watch the Thanksgiving Day Parade late in November that is staged by Macy's Department Store, the city's largest. The parade is a carnival of colour and noise with marching brass bands, vast floats and enormous balloon figures of famous television and children's book characters. This annual event, which began in 1924, has become less a celebration of Thanksgiving than the starting signal for the Christmas shopping season and so it is not unintentional that the parade comes to an end outside – where else – the main doors of Macy's.

One must turn to Central Park, however, to get a real idea of New Yorkers busy relaxing and there is no better way to do it than from the inside of one of the hansom cabs that can be hired at the Grand Army Plaza end of the park. Here on summertime Wednesday and Saturday mornings children's story tellings are held by the Hans Christian Andersen statue. On the other side of The Mall, in Sheep Meadow, the New York Philharmonic plays to crowds of up to 100,000 while at the Woolnan Rink rock concerts offer an equally well-attended alternative. The open-air stage of the Delacorte Theater is the venue of an annual 'pop-Shakespeare' Festival where Elizabethan drama becomes transformed by Brooklyn accents and sharp-tongued urban humour to something trendy but totally 'New York'. And, as if improved Shakespeare were not enough, a small section of the park called the Shakespeare Gardens has been devoted to nothing else but the botanical products referred to in his plays.

The traditional New York greeting for returning celebrities is a tickertape parade through the city streets. Here, Apollo astronauts are welcomed back from their trip to the moon.

Above: A scene by The Belvedere, about 1900, when Central Park was still *the* place to be seen taking a walk, or preferably riding or driving a coach. Until 1899 cars were banned from the park.

Right: The 843-acre rectangle of Central Park, which has been called New York's 'green lung', is one of the few places in the city where New Yorkers can relax, away from the hustle and bustle of the crowded streets.

Central Park also has a delightful zoo. It is a favourite place of lunching New Yorkers, although strolling and eating is such a widespread habit in the city that it must not be mistaken as having any bearing on the time of day.

More spectacular, and just as enjoyable, is the enormous Bronx Zoo with its 3000 inhabitants and a staggering food bill to match. Here you can thrill to the sight of a real Afro-Bronx game park where the animals are allowed to wander in 'safe-areas' rather than be enclosed in cages.

Right: Summertime brings crowds of youngsters flooding to see the marionette theatre in Central Park.

Below: The stone chess tables of Central Park attract a steady flow of dedicated enthusiasts seeking fresh air and concentration. Several hundred such tables are scattered in parks around the city.

Above: Patches of greenery abound in New York, but they take some finding. New Yorkers make use of every inch of free space to tend their little plots.

FREE
PUPPET
SHOWS

12:30
HANSEL
AND
GRETEL

1:45 MENTALLY
MARVELOUS

Left: A perennial favourite for tourists and natives alike is the ferry ride to the Statue of Liberty. The trip across the harbour affords a superb view of the city skyline and a glimpse of the more than 700 miles of dockland.

Below: The evening of Independence Day, July 4th, is celebrated with a magnificent display of fireworks over the East River.

The Lights of Broadway

The pulse of New York quickens at night when the blaze of lights that illuminate the city give it a renewed surge of energy, like some fresh flow of adrenalin. Not only Broadway, but every one of the bustling main avenues becomes transformed into a 'Great White Way' vibrating with life and excitement.

The heartbeat of New York's nightlife pulses — at least in myth — around the entertainment district of Broadway. Here, in the immediate neighbourhood of Time Square are some 36 theatres. In actual fact, very few are on Broadway itself and the majority cluster in the side streets between Broadway and Eighth Avenue and 44th to 53rd streets. Every year, on average, some 70 new productions open on Broadway; quite a staggering figure in these days of escalating costs and shrinking attendance figures. But Broadway is showbusiness — the term very faithfully captures the American approach to entertainment — and like all businesses must have plenty of new products to sell.

In Times Square there stands a statue of the Irish songwriter, George Cohan, who immortalized the entire area with his famous 'Give My Regards to Broadway' melody. The song is an odd blend of the overblown sentimentality that seems to go hand in hand with the brash, glittering face of Broadway and the ruthless and often cynical business practices that prevail behind the scenes. Still, credit must be given where it is due. Cohan, and other writers like him, did manage to give 42nd Street, one of the least romantic names imaginable, a genuine magic of its own. Unfortunately, 42nd Street has come down a long way over the years. Today it is a rather sleazy strip of porn cinemas and related cultural delights.

New York theatre life does not just begin and end with Broadway. A thriving 'off-Broadway' tradition (New Yorkese for Greenwich Village) survives in that part of town where there are some 20 or so well-established theatres presenting a great deal of the most exciting new work to emerge in America. Theatres located elsewhere in the city tend to be lumped as 'Off-off Broadway'. The term tends to describe their place in the financial pecking order as well.

The mid-town theatre district is also filled with dozens of restaurants and clubs that tend to be rather expensive. Yet these are the watering-holes of the rich and the famous who come to New York to be seen from all the world over. The parade of expensive limousines making their way east after the theatres empty is as impressive today as it has always been.

Another style of nightlife flourishes down in Greenwich Village, long the 'Left Bank' or Bohemian district of the city. Here are found dozens of small cafes, restaurants and clubs, each selling its own specialized blend of culture. But whether a place is a jazz, rock or folk club (or any combination of the three) the distinct sound emerges from rather similar conditions. The clubs are cramped, smoky, low, dingy and, for the most part, jam-packed.

The throbbing heart of the night-time beast is New York's famous landmark, Times Square, here ablaze with light and life.

New York bars are very much institutions in their own right. In recent years there has been a minor cult in bars for specialist clienteles such as gay bars and singles bars – the latter are sometimes disparagingly termed 'meet-markets'. The typical New York bar, if there is such a thing, as typical, tends to be dark, intimate, somewhat over-refrigerated by the air-conditioning and serves what could easily be the best drinks in the world.

The cocktails are, inevitably, delicious and served by dedicated barmen who work with painstaking care and craftsmanship. Bars range from the very basic neighbourhood variety to the opulent plushness of the best hotels, where, in a time honoured tradition, a pianist will appear from time to time and tinkle the keys – just like a 1940s movie.

Below: What watches are to Switzerland, the chorus line of the Rockettes was to America – the ultimate in precision. They were the star attraction of Radio City Music Hall, which closed in 1978 after 45 years of business.

Above and below: Broadway, the 'Great White Way' of song and legend, as it looked at the turn of the century and as it does today, nearly 80 years later.

The sound of the city – in clubs throughout Manhattan, every variety of music can be sampled; from the new wave sound of Patti Smith to the country and western style of Dolly Parton.

More than Manhattan

For most of the world, New York is synonymous with Manhattan. To a visitor this may seem logical, but the average New Yorker is quite likely to feel otherwise. For a start, more New Yorkers live outside Manhattan than in it and a great many grudgingly regard it as thriving at their expense.

Manhattan is linked to the outer boroughs by a network of tunnels and bridges and even by ferry. Every morning millions of workers stream across the 16 bridges and through the four tunnels that connect Manhattan to the rest of the world, only to stream back across and through them and desert the island at night.

Brooklyn, an area of more than 76 square miles and numbering some three million inhabitants is virtually a city in its own right. Originally a low-lying marshland of cranberry thickets and birds, it is today a major shipbuilding centre. The borough is not without strife and the appalling slums of Brownsville offer a stark contrast to the elegant dwellings on Brooklyn Heights. Places of interest include the 520 acre, meticulously landscaped Prospect Park, the Botanic Gardens with their section for the blind where plant descriptions are in braille, the Brooklyn Museum and a special Children's Museum.

The longest suspension bridge in the world, the Verrazano-Narrows Bridge, joins Brooklyn to Staten Island. The island lies five miles from Manhattan out in the Upper Bay. It can also be reached by a 20 minute ferry ride from the Battery at the tip of Manhattan which affords a splendid view of the financial district and the Statue of Liberty. This is one of the cheapest ways to enjoy the scenery of the city. The highest point on the 58 square miles of Staten Island is the 410 feet-high Todt Hill. Richmond, once the main town of Staten Island, is well worth visiting to see the authentic 17th-century village which includes one of the oldest schoolhouses in the United States. Also worth a visit is the Conference House at Tottenville where negotiations to end the War of Independence took place between the British and the Americans in 1776, and the house in Rosebank where the famous Italian freedom fighter Garibaldi lived.

To the northeast of Brooklyn lies the borough of Queens, established in the 17th century and patriotically named after the wife of King Charles II. By far the largest borough in New York, it encompasses an area of 121 square miles. Queens is the site of Kennedy Airport, with its 30 miles of runways for international flights, and La Guardia Airport from where domestic flights originate. Queens is also a great centre for leisure activities and is the site of Forest Hill Tennis Stadium and Shea Stadium where up to 80,000 spectators can enjoy football and baseball games. For nature lovers, there are the beautiful Rockaway Beaches in the south and the famous Jamaica Bay Wildlife Refuge, the largest urban nature reserve in the world.

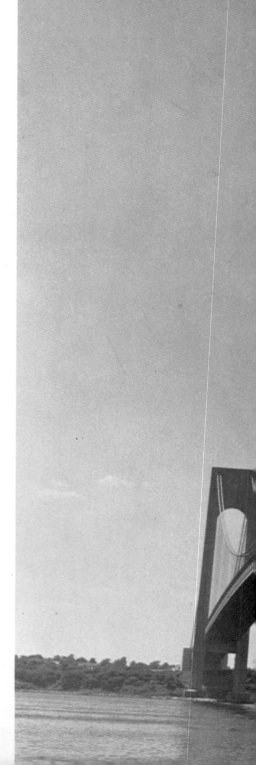

The world's longest suspension bridge, and New York's newest, is the Verrazano-Narrows Bridge that spans the channel connecting the harbour to the Atlantic Ocean.

New York's northernmost borough is the Bronx, named after the
Danish immigrant Johannes Bronck's 500 acre farm that once existed
here. The Bronx, with its population of more than a million and a half,
is a rather delapidated suburb yet it boasts a large expanse of green in
Van Cortlandt Park. Well worth a visit are the New York Botanical
Gardens with their splendid collection of tropical and wild flowers, and
the Bronx Zoo – the largest in the United States with 3000 animals. The
famous Yankee Stadium which accommodates up to 54,000 sports
fans is also of interest if for no other reason than it being the home of
the 'Bronx cheer'.

Of all the boroughs, perhaps the Bronx has the most traumatic
problems. As the middle classes have fled the area and the tenement
sections have been left to decay, parts of the Bronx have acquired an
almost lunar landscape of gutted and abandoned buildings. Arson, the
most recent blight, accounts for some 30 fires a night.

Manhattan, home of the city administration, has often been accused
of self interest by its satellite boroughs. But strong local loyalties
continue to exist, even in the face of the now all too familiar urban
problems, and the outer boroughs still have much of interest for the
visitor to New York.

Below left: La Guardia airport in northern Queens today handles all domestic flights, sharing the air traffic with John F. Kennedy International Airport.
Right: The sprawling waterfront installations of Brooklyn are the location of one of the world's great shipbuilding industries.
Below: The magnificent Bronx Zoo is laid out in an 'open-plan' arrangement that allows animals great freedom of movement.

Left: The extensive network of bays and rivers that intersect Greater New York afford plenty of opportunity for boating.
Right: Brooklyn and Queens are dotted with housing projects designed specifically for lower or middle income families. Others are purpose built for bachelors or the retired and semi-retired. They are often complete miniature towns in their own right.
Below: Jones Beach on the Atlantic Ocean, visible here beyond its open-air marine theatre, is one of a number of superb beaches within a short distance of downtown New York.

Away from it All

Ringed as it is by an expressway and linked to the rest of the world by some 20 bridges and tunnels and a network of fast roads, escape from Manhattan is a simple matter. An hour's drive from the centre of town can leave you deep in the country or, for that matter, standing in a traffic jam in the endless suburbs of Long Island – you have to choose your route with care.

The Atlantic is within easy reach of New York at a number of places, the nearest of of all being in Long Island. Here there are dozens of beaches. Those to the south are sandy and directly on the Atlantic while the ones to the north are shingle and face the Long Island Sound. Closest to the heart of the city is Coney Island at the southern tip of Brooklyn, and still on the subway line. Here is found one of the most spectacular amusement parks in the country. It is also the home of a hotdog of the same name covered with a delicious spicy sauce.

Further east, on the long finger of land belonging to Queens that borders the Atlantic, are the Rockaway Beaches, the only places in New York City to have good surfing. Continuing in the same direction to Wantaugh on Long Island one arrives at Jones Beach State Park. It has one of the busiest beaches on the entire East Coast with facilities to accomodate more than 100,000 bathers. In addition to swimming and fishing, there is a two-mile boardwalk, numerous restaurants and a Marine theatre where water-show spectaculars are staged.

Many New Yorkers, when they speak of leaving the city, immediately think of making their way to the beautiful rolling countryside that lies to the north. A delightful day's excursion is a trip along either side of the Hudson River Valley

After leaving Manhattan, drive north along the east side of the river toward Lyndhurst, one of the many fabulous riverside mansions that were erected here in the 19th century. Built in 1835 by William Pauling and later purchased by the notorious railway tycoon Jay Gould, this rambling gothic revival castle is today a museum cluttered with expensive furniture and tapestries of every description. The house is set in a magnificent 67 acre parkland of woods, gardens and greenhouses. In July and August every year, outdoor concerts are held here.

To the north one passes the Philpsburg Manor, an early 18th-century manor house and mill. Further on is the Old Dutch Church of Sleepy Hollow, the region where Washington Irving set his famous *Legend of Sleepy Hollow*. Throughout this area are numerous other estates such as Caramoor and Bosobel, although both are surpassed by the extraordinary Dick's Hilltop Castle, an actual model (though unfinished) of the Alhambra in Spain. The money ran out before it was completed, proving that even American millionaires have bottoms to their pockets. The sumptuous Vanderbilt Mansion and Hyde Park, the home of President Franklin D. Roosevelt, are also found in this region.

In summer, the beach and spectacular amusement park at Coney Island draw New Yorkers by the thousands seeking to escape the muggy heat of the city.

The drive along the west bank of the Hudson is less mansioned but equally pleasant. The road leads through Bear Mountain State Park, an expanse of lake and forest wilderness barely 40 miles from mid-town Manhattan. To the north of the park lies West Point, the famous academy for future American military leaders, and Washingtonville, the site of the country's oldest winery. Here too is Duchess County, famous for its long tradition of antique auctions. The dealers here trade almost exclusively in country-style furnishings (called Americana) of every description. Auctions are usually at the weekends.

To the north are the Catskill Mountains, New York's year round playground. This beautiful region abounds with luxury hotels and resorts providing every holiday diversion from sports to big-name nightclub acts. It is even rumoured that one of the best hotels employs a staff psychiatrist for New Yorkers who cannot bear to leave the madness of the city behind.

Right: The thoroughbred races at Saratoga Springs, a town also famous for its spa, were once a 'must' event in the social calendar of New York society.
Below right: Between the state capital of Albany and New York City, the Hudson River flows through almost Rhine-like scenery.
Below: Stifling humidity drives New Yorkers out of the city each summer to the fresh air of the Catskill and Adirondack Mountains.

Above: Central New York State, a country of rolling mountain wilderness, is but a few hours travel from downtown Manhattan.
Right: To the north of the Hudson Valley lies the meandering expanse of Lake George, long a favourite summer resort of New Yorkers.